The Date of the Resurrection
Sunday, 3 April 33

Madeleine et les saintes femmes au tombeau.
Painting by James Tissot (1836-1902).

Decio Martins de Medeiros
São Paulo – Brasil – 2024

This is a translation of the original in Portuguese: A data da Ressurreição.

Bibliographic Information:
Author: Decio Martins de Medeiros
Title: The Date of the Resurrection
Subtitle: Sunday, 3 April, 33
Place, Year: São Paulo, Brazil, 2024
Pages: 79 pages, 6"x9" size
Illustrations by: James Tissot (1836–1902)
Subjects: 1. Christianity 2. History

Table of Contents

Preface..5
Calendar Conversion 7
Chronology of Christ's Life................................9
Herod I died on 14 of January of 1 CE.............32
Year Zero – Christmas One................................34
Consuls, Olympics, Race Winners......................41
Beginning of the Public Life of Christ 44
The Dates of the Jewish Passover....................46
The Jewish Passovers During the Public Life..........48
The Last Supper on Thursday...........................50
The Crucifixion on Friday.................................52
The Burial on Friday 56
The Sabbath of the Jewish Passover................58
The Sunday of Christ's Resurrection.................60
The moon in April of 33..................................63
The Earthquake in April of 33..........................66
The Dates of Christian Easter..........................69
The Ancient Traditions.....................................73
Faith in the Resurrection of the Whole Person......74
Justice, Altruism, Charity 76
About the Author...78

<u>Illustrations by James Tissot (1836-1902)</u>

The cover features the painting depicting Mary Magdalene and the women on their first visit to Christ's tomb on the morning of the Resurrection.[1]

Other paintings by James Tissot can be found in various museums and galleries.[2]

---

[1] https://www.brooklynmuseum.org/opencollection/objects/13518
[2] https://www.brooklynmuseum.org/opencollection/artists/142/objects
https://www.metmuseum.org/art/collection/search#!/search?artist=Tissot,%20James$James%20Tissot
https://www.globalgallery.com/product/T/James_Tissot/

Preface

My previous book *Year Zero – Christmas One* addresses several questions about our calendar and some events that marked the beginning of year counting.

Does our calendar, known as the Gregorian calendar, have a year zero? In December of year zero, how old was Christ? And did Herod die before year zero, as some historians claim? How can we verify that our calendar is accurate?

The book confirms the validity of the current calendar based on unprecedented chronological research conducted in 2016. Using the solar calendar revealed by the Dead Sea Scrolls, the study demonstrates synchronization with six other events: one annual, two specific, and three millennial—astronomical in March, historical in 70 AD, biblical in 2 BC, Christian festivals in June and December, and the Jewish circumcision ceremony!

Following the confirmation in *Year Zero – Christmas One* that our current Gregorian calendar is correct and that Jesus was born on 25 December, 1 BC, this book will establish the date of Christ's Resurrection on Sunday, 3 April, 33 AD, when He was just over 33 years old. This book explores the events of that Sunday, which occurred after the full moon following the March equinox. The event was preceded by a lunar eclipse, accompanied by an earthquake, and is supported by biblical and historical records, as well as the millennia-old tradition of celebrating Good Friday and Resurrection Sunday.

All dates mentioned are in the Gregorian calendar unless another calendar is indicated.

Calendar Conversion

The topic of calendars is quite extensive in itself. For the purposes of this book, it is sufficient to understand the conversion between the Gregorian, Julian, Hebrew, and Roman calendars.

The Gregorian calendar has a year zero, but the Julian calendar does not have a year zero. The Gregorian year zero is the year minus one, also referred to as 1 BC, in the Julian calendar.

For date conversion between the Hebrew, Julian, Gregorian, and Julian Day calendars, refer to the website http://www.fourmilab.ch/documents/calendar/

Anno Periodi Juliani is equal to Julian Day divided by 365.25.

1 AUC starts on April 21, -753 (Gregorian) and ends on April 20, -752 (Gregorian).
754 AUC starts on April 21, 0 (Gregorian) and ends on April 20, 1 (Gregorian).

For the calendar of the time, including the phases of the moon, see
http://www.paulcarlisle.net/mooncalendar/

Other websites presenting lunar phases:

https://webspace.science.uu.nl/~gent0113/easter/easter_text2a.htm

https://www.moongiant.com/calendar/april/2025/

http://astropixels.com/ephemeris/phasescat/phases2001.html

https://eclipse.gsfc.nasa.gov/SKYCAL/SKYCAL.html

Chronology of Christ's Life

Birth of Christ – Painting by James Tissot

This chronological study of Christ's life begins with the event in which the Jewish priest Zacharias, while serving in the Temple of Jerusalem, learned that he would become the father of John the Baptist. The final event in this chronological study is the 20th year of the reign of Tiberius Caesar.

Based on the Dead Sea Scrolls and the historical record of the Temple's destruction in August 70 AD, it has been possible to date Zacharias' event to September 2 BC, and from there confirm Christ's birth in December 1 BC. Other historical, biblical, and astronomical information allows for the construction of the chronology up to the Resurrection on April 3, 33 AD.

Some historians have incorrectly dated the death of Herod I to 4 BC, creating confusion in the chronology of Christ. Fortunately, later studies corrected this error and confirmed Herod's death in 1 AD.

In this chronology, I use the following abbreviations:

BC = Before Christ = BCE = Before Common Era
AD = Anno Domini (After Christ) = CE = Common Era
G = Gregorian calendar
J = Julian calendar
H = Hebrew calendar
AUC = Roman calendar

AUC:752 from 21/April/-2G to 20/April/-1G

G: 21/September/-2
J : 23/September/-3
H: 14/Tishri/3759
Zechariah receives the announcement of the conception of John the Baptist while he was serving in the Temple, during the duty shift of the class of Abias. [3] [4]

G: 03/February/-1
J: 05/February/-2
H: 01/Adar/3759
Augustus Caesar Receives the Title of Pater Patriae.
In *Res Gestae* Part V, Item 35, written by Augustus himself, he states, "While I was administering my thirteenth consulship, the Senate, the Equestrian Order, and all the Romans gave me the title of Father of the Fatherland..." [5]

G: 23/March/-1
J: 25/March/-2
H: 20/Nisan/3759

---

[3] Luke 1,5; Luke 1,8; Luke 1,11; Luke 1,13; Luke 1,23.

[4] https://play.google.com/store/books/details/Decio_Martins_de_Medeiros_Year_Zero_Christmas_One?id=DxQUEQAAQBAJ

[5] http://penelope.uchicago.edu/Thayer/E/Roman/Texts/Augustus/Res_Gestae/6*.html

Mary of Nazareth receives the announcement of the conception of Jesus Christ six months after Zechariah received the announcement of the conception of John the Baptist. [6]

---

[6] Luke 1,25; Luke 1,31; Luke 1,36

G: 10/May/-1
J : 12/May/-2
H: 09/Sivan/3759
Augustus Caesar inaugurates the Forum of Augustus, and the dedication of the Forum and the Temple of Mars takes place on 01/August/-2, according to the Julian calendar. [7] [8] [9]

G: 15/June/-1
J: 17/June/-2
H: 15/Tammuz/3759
Star of Bethlehem: On August 10, 2 BC, according to the Gregorian calendar, the two brightest planets in the Solar System, Venus and Jupiter, came very close to each other, with only 4.3 arcseconds of separation, appearing almost to touch. Ten months later, on June 15, 1 BC, Venus and Jupiter approached again, this time with only 0.5 arcseconds of separation, so that, to the naked eye, they appeared as a single "star." (Bidelman 1991) The "Star" appeared twice: on August 10, 2 BC, before the Magi set out, and on June 15, 1 BC, when they arrived.[10] On June 17, 2 BC, according

---

[7] C. Velleius Paterculus, The Roman History, Loeb Classical Library 1924. book 2, chapter 100, item 2

[8] Cassius Dio, book LV item 10; book LX item 5.3

[9] H. Jordan, Topographie der Stadt Rom in Altertum. Vol. I, Parts I, 2; Vol. II. Berlin 1871 1885, page 444

[10] http://ed5015.tripod.com/BChristmasStar81.html

to the Julian calendar, there was a Full Moon.[11]

G: 22/June/-1
J: 24/June/-2
H: 22/Tammuz/3759
John the Baptist is born nine months after the announcement to Zechariah.

Quirinius was governor of Syria in 3 BC, 2 BC, AD 6, and AD 7, according to the Julian calendar.[12]
Quirinius conducts his first census.[13]
Quintus Aemilius Secundus leaves a record mentioning a census by Quirinius:

"Q[uintus] Aemilius Secundus, son of Q[uintus], of the Palatine tribe, who served in the camps of the divine Aug[ustus] under P. Sulpicius Quirinius, legate of Caesar in Syria, decorated with honorary distinctions, prefect of the 1st Aug[usta] cohort, prefect of the 2nd Classica cohort. Additionally, by order of Quirinius, I conducted the census in Apamea of 117,000 male citizens. Moreover, sent on a mission by Quirinius, against the Itureans, on Mount Lebanon, I took their citadel. And before military service, (I was) Prefect of workers, appointed by two co[nsul]s in the 'aerarium

---

[11] http://www.paulcarlisle.net/mooncalendar/
[12] James A. Nollet, Astronomical and Historical Evidence for Dating the Nativity in 2 BC, in Perspectives on Science and Christian Faith, Volume 64, Number 4, December 2012 , pages 211-219
[13] Luke 2,2

[The State Treasury]'..."[14]

Mary, who was pregnant, and Joseph traveled up to Bethlehem in Judea to be registered, fulfilling the decree issued by Augustus Caesar, calling the population of the empire to be counted/registered.[15]

6,000 Jews refuse to swear allegiance to Augustus Caesar, one year before Herod's death.[16]

G: 25/December/-1
J : 27/December/-2
H: 01/Shevat/3760
Jesus Christ is born nine months after the announcement to Mary.[17]

G: 01/January/0
J : 03/January/-1
H:08/Shevat/3760
Christ receives the name Jesus during the Jewish religious ceremony of circumcision on the eighth day counting from the day of His birth.[18] [19] Start of the

---

[14] book Inscriptiones latinae selectae by Hermann Dessau, published in 1892, in item 2683
https://archive.org/details/inscriptioneslat01dessuoft
[15] Luke 2,1-11
[16] Flavius Josephus, Antiquities of the Jews, Book 17, Chapter 2, Section 4
[17] https://play.google.com/store/books/details?id=nSYEEAAAQBAJ
[18] Levíticus 12,3
[19] Luke 2,21

year zero of the Gregorian calendar.[20]

G: 02/February/0
J : 04/February/-1
H:10/Adar I/3760
Jesus was taken to Jerusalem after the forty days of purification for Mary were completed.[21]

G: 23/March/0
J: 25/March/-1
H:01/Nisan/3760
Herod completes his 36th year of reign and begins his 37th year of reign.

---

[20] http://www.cs.tau.ac.il/~nachum/calendar-book/third-edition/
[21] Luke 2,22

AUC: 754 from 21/April/0G to 20/April/1G

G: 21/April/0
J: 23/April/-1
H: 30/Nisan/3760
Rome completes 753 years since its founding on 21/April/-753 (Gregorian calendar). Beginning of the year 754 AUC, from 21/April/0 to 20/April/1 of the Gregorian calendar.

G: 25/December/0
J : 27/December/-1
H:11/Tevet/3761
Jesus Christ turns 1 year old. Check the proof in the book Year Zero – Christmas One. [22]

G: 29/December/0
J : 31/December/-1
H:15/Tevet/3761
Full Moon has a visible eclipse in Jerusalem at 5:02 PM with 53% totality.[23] [24] [25] [26]

---

[22] https://play.google.com/store/books/details?id=nSYEEAAAQBAJ

[23] https://eclipse.gsfc.nasa.gov/LEcat5/LE-0099-0000.html#1

[24] James A. Nollet, Astronomical and Historical Evidence for Dating the Nativity in 2 BC, in Perspectives on Science and Christian Faith, Volume 64, Number 4, December 2012 , pages 211-219

[25] Theodor vol Oppolzer, Canon of Eclipses, supplemented by Jean Meeus, Catalogue of Lunar Eclipses.

[26] http://www.paulcarlisle.net/mooncalendar/

G: 30/December/0
J : 01/January/1
H: 16/Tevet/3761
Caius/Gaius Julius Caesar became one of the two consuls of the Roman Empire, beginning his term on 1/January/1 of the Julian calendar.[27]
Flavius Josephus states that Caius/Gaius Caesar was in Rome after the death of Herod.[28]

G: 01/January/1
J : 03/January/1
H:18/Tevet/3761
Start of Year 1 of the Gregorian calendar.
The Gregorian calendar has a year zero, but the Julian calendar does not have a year zero.[29]
Varus was governor of Syria in 5 BC, 4 BC, 1 BC, and 1 AD, according to the Julian calendar.[30]

G: 30/December/0 till 26/March/1
J : 01/January/1 till 29/March/1
H:15/Tevet/3761 till 15/Nisan/3761
Herod the Great is in his final days of life:
Herod's illness worsens.[31]

---

[27] https://en.wikipedia.org/wiki/List_of_Roman_consuls#1st_century_BC

[28] Flavius Josephus- Antiquities of the Jews. Book 17, chapter 9, paragraph 5.

[29] http://www.cs.tau.ac.il/~nachum/calendar-book/third-edition/

[30] James A. Nollet, Astronomical and Historical Evidence for Dating the Nativity in 2 BC, in Perspectives on Science and Christian Faith, Volume 64, Number 4, December 2012 , pages 211-219

[31] Flavius Josephus - Wars I 33:1,5

He is taken for treatment with hot baths 15 km away and then returned.[32]
Herod planned his own funeral.[33]
Herod summoned important men from each village, up to 130 kilometers away, and they came.[34]
Antipater, one of Herod's sons, is executed, and Herod dies five days later.[35]

G: 14/January/1
J: 16/January/1
H: 02/Shevat/3761
Jewish holiday commemorates the death of Herod on the second day of Shevat.[36] [37] [38] [39]
Herod's body was carried 35 kilometers from Jericho to Herodium by soldiers who walked a mile a day, and then it was buried.[40]
Seven days of mourning followed, and then feast. [41]
Another public mourning was held by some patriots

---

[32] Flavius Josephus - Wars I 33:5-6; Antiquities XVII 6:5
[33] Flavius Josephus - Wars I 33:6
[34] Flavius Josephus - Antiquities XVII 6:5
[35] Flavius Josephus - Wars I 33:7-8; Antiquities XVII 7;8:1
[36] http://www.setterfield.org/star_technical.html
[37] Codex Judaica – Chronological Index of Jewish History – Zichron Press – New York – 2005 page 132
[38] The Jewish Time Line Encyclopedia: A Year-by-Year History From Creation to the Present por Mattis Kantor , Rowan & Littlefield Publishers, Inc –USA-1992 page 92
[39] Supplementary Dissertation in the book The Fulness of the Times: Being an Analysis of the Chronology of the Seventy, by William Cuninghame. London, 1837 page 18
[40] Flavius Josephus - Antiquities XVII 8:3
[41] Flavius Josephus - Wars II 1:1; Antiquities XVII 8:4

before the eclipse.[42]
Archelaus, one of Herod's sons, is crowned and issues some decrees before Pesach.[43]

G: 13/March/1
J:15/March/1
H:01/Nisan/3761
Herod would complete his 37th year of reign.
This 37th year of reign is considered based on the correlation that Josephus made between the 7th year of Herod's reign and the year of the Battle of Actium.[44]
[45]

G: 26/March/1
J :29/March/1
H:15/Nisan/3761
Jews celebrate the Pesach festival, which begins on the 15th of Nisan each year.[46]

---

[42] Flavius Josephus - Wars II 1:2
[43] Flavius Josephus - Wars I 33:8
[44] Flavius Josephus- War of the Jews,Book 1, Chapter19, item 3
[45] http://sacred-texts.com/jud/josephus/war-1.htm
[46] Flavius Josephus - Wars II 1:3; Antiquities XVII 9:3

AUC:755 from 21/April/1G to 20/April/2G

G: 29/June/ 1
J:01/July/1
H: 30/Tammuz/3761
Consuls of Rome: C. Caesar Aug. f. [Divi n.], [L. Aemilius Paulli f. L. n.] Paullus.
From July 1st: M. Herennius M. f. M'. n. Picens[47] [48]

---

[47] https://pt.wikipedia.org/wiki/Fastos_Capitolinos
[48] http://www.attalus.org/translate/fasti3.html

AUC:756 from 21/April/2G to 20/April/3G

G: 29/June/2
J: 01/July/2
H:02/Tammuz/3762
Consuls of Rome: P. Vinicius M. f. P. n., P. Alfenus P. f. P. n. Varus.
From July 1st: P. Cornelius Cn. f. Cn. n. Scipio, T. Quinctius T. f. T. n. [Crispinus] Valerianus.[49] [50]

---

[49] https://pt.wikipedia.org/wiki/Fastos_Capitolinos
[50] http://www.attalus.org/translate/fasti3.html

AUC:757 from 21/April/3G to 20/April/4G

....

AUC:758 from 21/April/4G to 20/April/5G

G: 24/June/4
J : 26/June/4
H: 19/Tammuz/3764
Augustus Caesar adopts his son-in-law Tiberius (the future Tiberius Caesar) as his son. Tiberius receives some powers.[51] [52] [53]

---

[51] http://www.roman-emperors.org/auggie.htm
[52] https://pt.wikipedia.org/wiki/Augusto
[53]

The Adoption of Agrippa Postumus and the Friends of Gaius Caesar in The Republic in Danger: Drusus Libo and the Succession of Tiberius. Author: Andrew Pettinger. Oxford Scholarship Online: September 2012.

AUC:759 from 21/April/5G to 20/April/6G

....

AUC:768 from 21/April/14G to 20/April/15G

G: 17/August/14
J: 19/August/14
H: 05/Elul/3774
Augustus Caesar dies in the 57th year of his
reign.[54] [55]

G: 16/September/14
J: 18/September/14
H:06/Tishri/3775
Tiberius is confirmed by the Senate as emperor.[56]

G: 30/December/14
J: 01/January/15
H: 22/Teveth/3775
Tiberius Caesar is in his 1st year of reign. [57]

---

[54] http://www.roman-emperors.org/auggie.htm
[55] https://pt.wikipedia.org/wiki/Augusto
[56] http://www.roman-emperors.org/tiberius.htm
[57] http://www.dec25th.info

AUC:769 from 21/April/15G to 20/April/16G

....

AUC:782 from 21/April/28G to 20/April/29G

G: 30/December/28
J:01/January/29
H: 27/Teveth/3789
Tiberius Caesar is in his 15th year of reign.[58]

G: 14/April/29
J: 16/April/29
H:14/Nisan/3789
Jews have on the 14th of Nisan the eve of the Feast of Pesach, the Jewish Passover.

---

[58] http://www.dec25th.info

AUC:783 from 21/April/29G to 20/April/30G

G: 06/November/29
J: 08/November/29
H: 13/Heshvan/3790
Jesus Christ, nearly 30 years old, is baptized by John the Baptist in the 15th year of Tiberius Caesar.[59]
Jesus was about thirty years old when he began His ministry.[60]

G: 25/December/29
J: 27/December/29
H: 03/Teveth/3790
As Jesus Christ turned 1 year old on 25/December/0 [61] so **Christ turned 30 years old on 25/December/29.**

G: 03/April/30
J: 05/April/30
H: 14/Nisan/3790
The Jews observe on the 14th of Nisan the eve of the Feast of Pesach, the Jewish Passover. 16th year of Tiberius Caesar.

---

[59] http://www.dec25th.info
[60] Luke 3,23
[61] https://www.barnesandnoble.com/w/year-zero-christmas-one-decio-martins-de-medeiros/1145514528

AUC:784 from 21/April/30G to 20/April/31G

G: 24/March/31
J: 26/March/31
H: 14/Nisan/3791
The Jews observe on the 14th of Nisan the eve of the Feast of Pesach, the Jewish Passover. 17th year of Tiberius Caesar.

AUC:785 from 21/April/31G to 20/April/32G

G: 12/April/32
J: 14/April/32
H: 14/Nisan/3792
The Jews observe on the 14th of Nisan the eve of the Feast of Pesach, the Jewish Passover. 18th year of Tiberius Caesar.

AUC:786 from 21/April/32G to 20/April/33G

G: 31/March/33 **Thursday**
J: 02/April/33
H: 13/Nisan/3793
After sunset on Thursday, the day of preparation for the Jewish Passover began, which extends through Friday until sunset.
Jesus and his disciples have the **Last Supper.**

G: 01/April/33 **Friday**
J: 03/April/33
H: 14/Nisan/3793
Crucifixion of Jesus Christ, at the age of 33 years and 3 months, on Friday, the eve of the Jewish Passover. Passover begins after sunset.
It is the 19th year of Tiberius Caesar. [62]

G: 02/April/33 **Saturday**
J: 04/April/33
H: 15/Nisan/3793
Pesach, the Jewish Passover.

---

[62] http://www.dec25th.info

G: 03/April/33 Sunday
J: 05/April/33
H: 16/Nisan/3793
Sunday of Christ's Resurrection.

AUC:787 from 21/April/33G to 20/April/34G

G: 30/December/33
J: 01/January/34
H: 13/Teveth/3794
Tiberius Caesar is in his 20th year of reign.

Herod I died on 14 of January of 1 CE.

So, did Herod die in 4 BCE or 1 CE?

We know that Herod was alive when Christ was born and that before he died, he ordered the massacre of all boys under 2 years old.

Which historical marker should we rely on: the date of Christ's birth or the date of Herod's death?

If Christ was born in December of 1 BCE in the Gregorian calendar, then the chronology shows that Herod must have died around 1 CE.

If Herod died in 4 BCE, then Christ would have had to be born around 6 BCE!!!

Jewish texts reveal that the date of Herod I the Great's death is 2 Shevat 3761 in the Hebrew calendar, which corresponds to January 14, 0001 in the Gregorian calendar.

Refer to page 132 of "Codex Judaica – Chronological Index of Jewish History – Zichron Press – New York – 2005."

Refer to page 92 of the book "The Jewish Time Line Encyclopedia: A Year-by-Year History From

Creation to the Present" edited by Mattis Kantor, Rowan & Littlefield Publishers, Inc – USA – 1992.

Refer to page 18 of the "Supplementary Dissertation" in the book "The Fullness of the Times: Being an Analysis of the Chronology of the Seventy" by William Cunningham. London, 1837.

Why have some recent historians begun to consider 4 BCE as the year of Herod's death? One of the "evidences" was coins indicating Herod's sons as his successors with dates earlier than previously thought. However, numismatists clarified that coins record "de jure" situations, not "de facto" situations. Herod the Great died in 1 CE, but his sons Herod Archelaus, Herod Antipas, and Herod Philip counted their Year 1 of reign from 4 BCE, which is when the "co-regency" of Antipater, one of Herod's sons, began.

In other words, the confusion arises because Herod allowed his son Antipater to co-rule with him and handle many public affairs.

Specifically regarding the error of dating Herod's death to 4 BCE, I suggest reading the articles by Vladimir Blaha on academia.edu.

Year Zero – Christmas One

On June 20, 2016, I completed and published the results of a research study on chronology and the date of Christ's birth. On May 15, 2017, they were published on the blog Prazer Compartilhar [63] [64] and subsequently on the site Academia.edu. [65]

On October 19, 2020, the book 'Ano Zero – Natal Um' was published [66], in partnership with my friend Carlos Fernando Castro, who created a fictional narrative to help illustrate the development of my research.

The objective of the research was to validate the current civil calendar, known as the Gregorian calendar, which counts AD from 01/January/0000, the eighth day after the birth of Christ on 25/December/year minus 1, seeking elements to substantiate this tradition that has reached us after more than two thousand years.

The 8-day difference between Christ's birth on December 25th, 1 BC, and the beginning of the New

---

[63]https://prazercompartilharblog.wordpress.com/2017/05/15/2-a-e-c-do-calendario-juliano-e-o-ano-de-nascimento-de-jesus-cristo/

[64]https://prazercompartilharblog.wordpress.com/2017/05/17/cronologia-ac-dc/

[65]
https://www.academia.edu/30100519/2_aec_do_calendario_Juliano_%C3%A9_o_ano_de_nascimento_de_Jesus_Cristo_pdf

[66] https://play.google.com/store/books/details?id=nSYEEAAAQBAJ

The Date of the Resurrection

Year on January 1st of year zero is due to the Jewish custom of naming a newborn on the eighth day after birth during the circumcision ritual. It was on January 1st of year zero that Christ was circumcised and given the name Jesus. Since Christ was born on December 25th, 1 BC, He was conceived around March 23rd, 1 BC, which was the time when Elizabeth, the relative of Mary, the mother of Jesus, was six months pregnant.

John the Baptist, the son of Elizabeth and Zechariah, was conceived around September 23rd, 2 BC. At that time, Zechariah was performing his priestly duties in the Temple. Zechariah belonged to the priestly division of Abias, one of the 24 divisions listed in 1 Chronicles 24:7-19. The priestly service schedule in the Temple follows a 6-year cycle with 52 weeks each year, according to the Qumran manuscripts.

week	1st year	2nd year	3rd year	4th year	5th year	6th year
1	22.Gamul	2.Jedeias	6.Mainã	10.Sequenias	14.Isbaal	18.Hafses
2	23.Dalaías	3.Harim	7.Acos	11.Eliasib	15.Belga	19.Fetatias
3	24.Maazias	4.Seorim	8.Abias	12.Jacim	16.Emer	20.Esequiel
4	1.Joiarib	5.Melquias	9.Jesua	13.Hofa	17.Hezir	21.Jaquin
5	2.Jedeias	6.Mainã	10.Sequenias	14.Isbaal	18.Hafses	22.Gamul
6	3.Harim	7.Acos	11.Eliasib	15.Belga	19.Fetatias	23.Dalaías
7	4.Seorim	8.Abias	12.Jacim	16.Emer	20.Esequiel	24.Maazias
8	5.Melquias	9.Jesua	13.Hofa	17.Hezir	21.Jaquin	1.Joiarib
9	6.Mainã	10.Sequenias	14.Isbaal	18.Hafses	22.Gamul	2.Jedeias
10	7.Acos	11.Eliasib	15.Belga	19.Fetatias	23.Dalaías	3.Harim
11	8.Abias	12.Jacim	16.Emer	20.Esequiel	24.Maazias	4.Seorim

The Date of the Resurrection

12	9.Jesua	13.Hofa	17.Hezir	21.Jaquin	1.Joiarib	5.Melquias
13	10.Sequenias	14.Isbaal	18.Hafses	22.Gamul	2.Jedeias	6.Mainã
14	11.Eliasib	15.Belga	19.Fetatias	23.Dalaías	3.Harim	7.Acos
15	12.Jacim	16.Emer	20.Esequiel	24.Maazias	4.Seorim	8.Abias
16	13.Hofa	17.Hezir	21.Jaquin	1.Joiarib	5.Melquias	9.Jesua
17	14.Isbaal	18.Hafses	22.Gamul	2.Jedeias	6.Mainã	10.Sequenias
18	15.Belga	19.Fetatias	23.Dalaías	3.Harim	7.Acos	11.Eliasib
19	16.Emer	20.Esequiel	24.Maazias	4.Seorim	8.Abias	12.Jacim
20	17.Hezir	21.Jaquin	1.Joiarib	5.Melquias	9.Jesua	13.Hofa
21	18.Hafses	22.Gamul	2.Jedeias	6.Mainã	10.Sequenias	14.Isbaal
22	19.Fetatias	23.Dalaías	3.Harim	7.Acos	11.Eliasib	15.Belga
23	20.Esequiel	24.Maazias	4.Seorim	8.Abias	12.Jacim	16.Emer
24	21.Jaquin	1.Joiarib	5.Melquias	9.Jesua	13.Hofa	17.Hezir
25	22.Gamul	2.Jedeias	6.Mainã	10.Sequenias	14.Isbaal	18.Hafses
26	23.Dalaías	3.Harim	7.Acos	11.Eliasib	15.Belga	19.Fetatias
27	24.Maazias	4.Seorim	8.Abias	12.Jacim	16.Emer	20.Esequiel
28	1.Joiarib	5.Melquias	9.Jesua	13.Hofa	17.Hezir	21.Jaquin
29	2.Jedeias	6.Mainã	10.Sequenias	14.Isbaal	18.Hafses	22.Gamul
30	3.Harim	7.Acos	11.Eliasib	15.Belga	19.Fetatias	23.Dalaías
31	4.Seorim	8.Abias	12.Jacim	16.Emer	20.Esequiel	24.Maazias
32	5.Melquias	9.Jesua	13.Hofa	17.Hezir	21.Jaquin	1.Joiarib
33	6.Mainã	10.Sequenias	14.Isbaal	18.Hafses	22.Gamul	2.Jedeias
34	7.Acos	11.Eliasib	15.Belga	19.Fetatias	23.Dalaías	3.Harim
35	8.Abias	12.Jacim	16.Emer	20.Esequiel	24.Maazias	4.Seorim
36	9.Jesua	13.Hofa	17.Hezir	21.Jaquin	1.Joiarib	5.Melquias
37	10.Sequenias	14.Isbaal	18.Hafses	22.Gamul	2.Jedeias	6.Mainã
38	11.Eliasib	15.Belga	19.Fetatias	23.Dalaías	3.Harim	7.Acos
39	12.Jacim	16.Emer	20.Esequiel	24.Maazias	4.Seorim	8.Abias
40	13.Hofa	17.Hezir	21.Jaquin	1.Joiarib	5.Melquias	9.Jesua
41	14.Isbaal	18.Hafses	22.Gamul	2.Jedeias	6.Mainã	10.Sequenias

The Date of the Resurrection

42	15.Belga	19.Fetatias	23.Dalaías	3.Harim	7.Acos	11.Eliasib
43	16.Emer	20.Esequiel	24.Maazias	4.Seorim	8.Abias	12.Jacim
44	17.Hezir	21.Jaquin	1.Joiarib	5.Melquias	9.Jesua	13.Hofa
45	18.Hafses	22.Gamul	2.Jedeias	6.Mainã	10.Sequenias	14.Isbaal
46	19.Fetatias	23.Dalaías	3.Harim	7.Acos	11.Eliasib	15.Belga
47	20.Esequiel	24.Maazias	4.Seorim	8.Abias	12.Jacim	16.Emer
48	21.Jaquin	1.Joiarib	5.Melquias	9.Jesua	13.Hofa	17.Hezir
49	22.Gamul	2.Jedeias	6.Mainã	10.Sequenias	14.Isbaal	18.Hafses
50	23.Dalaías	3.Harim	7.Acos	11.Eliasib	15.Belga	19.Fetatias
51	24.Maazias	4.Seorim	8.Abias	12.Jacim	16.Emer	20.Esequiel
52	1.Joiarib	5.Melquias	9.Jesua	13.Hofa	17.Hezir	21.Jaquin

The Date of the Resurrection

Scholars of the Qumran manuscripts have concluded that the Jewish sect living there synchronized each year of the priestly service schedule with the March equinox. They also concluded that, according to the priestly service schedule in the Temple, the March equinox in the Jerusalem time zone marks the first day of the first month. For the priestly service schedule in the Temple, the first month is the month of Nisan in the Hebrew calendar, which corresponds to the month of March in the Gregorian calendar. The first day of the first month of the year is the day following the day of the March equinox (which is designated as the 4th day of the service week).

We know that on August 3rd of the year 70, equivalent to 10th of Av 3830 in the Hebrew calendar, the Temple was destroyed for the second time. The priests of the Joiarib division were on duty in the Temple. Knowing that each year the service schedule is synchronized with the March equinox, and knowing that in August of the year 70 the Joiarib division was on duty in the Temple, by consulting the schedule, we see that in the third year of the six-year cycle, the Joiarib division is on duty in the Temple in August. Therefore, for the year 70, the schedule was in the third year of the six-year cycle.

Knowing that the year 70 was the third year of the six-year cycle, and tracing the six-year cycle of the service schedule, we see that the year 2 BC was also the third year of the six-year cycle.

We then confirm that on the annual Temple service schedule in the year 2 BC, the division of Abias, to which Zechariah belonged, was serving in the Temple at the end of September!

Thus, tradition, biblical references, historical records, and astronomical events have helped to confirm that Jesus Christ was born on December 25th, 1 BC, died on Friday, April 1st, 33, and resurrected on Sunday, April 3rd, 33. All dates are according to the Gregorian calendar!

Service schedule at the Temple by the priestly classes according to manuscripts 4Q320 and 4Q321.

Day following the March equinox is the 4th day of the service week and is also the 1st day of the 1st month.

The week of the priestly class begins on the evening of the day before the first day of the week.

3rd year of the 6-year cycle							Year 2 B.C. in the Gregorian calendar. Equinox: Saturday, March 21st.			
Week	Mo	1st day	Mo	7th day	Class		Month	Thu	Month	Wed
1	12	29	1	4	Maina		March 2 b.C.	19	March	25
2	1	5	1	11	Acos		March	26	April	1
3	1	12	1	18	Abias		April	2	April	8
4	1	19	1	25	Jesua		April	9	April	15
5	1	26	2	2	Sequenias		April	16	April	22
6	2	3	2	9	Eliasib		April	23	April	29
7	2	10	2	16	Jacim		April	30	May	6
8	2	17	2	23	Hofa		May	7	May	13
9	2	24	2	30	Isbaab		May	14	May	20
10	3	1	3	7	Belga		May	21	May	27
11	3	8	3	14	Emer		May	28	June	3
12	3	15	3	21	Hezir		June	4	June	10
13	3	22	3	28	Hafses		June	11	June	17
14	3	29	4	4	Fetatias		June	18	June	24
15	4	5	4	11	Ezequiel		June	25	July	1
16	4	12	4	18	Jaquin		July	2	July	8
17	4	19	4	25	Gamul		July	9	July	15
18	4	26	5	2	Dalaias		July	16	July	22
19	5	3	5	9	Maazias		July	23	July	29
20	5	10	5	16	Joairib		July	30	August	5
21	5	17	5	23	Jedeias		August	6	August	12
22	5	24	5	30	Harim		August	13	August	19
23	6	1	6	7	Seorim		August	20	August	26
24	6	8	6	14	Melquias		August	27	September	2
25	6	15	6	21	Maina		September	3	September	9
26	6	22	6	28	Acos		September	10	September	16
27	6	29	7	4	Abias	>>>	September	17	September	23
28	7	5	7	11	Jesua		September	24	September	30
29	7	12	7	18	Sequenias		October	1	October	7
30	7	19	7	25	Eliasib		October	8	October	14
31	7	26	8	2	Jacim		October	15	October	21
32	8	3	8	9	Hofa		October	22	October	28
33	8	10	8	16	Isbaab		October	29	November	4
34	8	17	8	23	Belga		November	5	November	11
35	8	24	8	30	Emer		November	12	November	18
36	9	1	9	7	Hezir		November	19	November	25
37	9	8	9	14	Hafses		November	26	December	2
38	9	15	9	21	Fetatias		December	3	December	9
39	9	22	9	28	Ezequiel		December	10	December	16
40	9	29	10	4	Jaquin		December	17	December	23
41	10	5	10	11	Gamul		December	24	December	30
42	10	12	10	18	Dalaias		December	31	January 1 a.C.	6
43	10	19	10	25	Maazias		January	7	January	13
44	10	26	11	2	Joairib		January	14	January	20
45	11	3	11	9	Jedeias		January	21	January	27
46	11	10	11	16	Harim		January	28	February	3
47	11	17	11	23	Seorim		February	4	February	10
48	11	24	11	30	Melquias		February	11	February	17
49	12	1	12	7	Maina		February	18	February	24
50	12	8	12	14	Acos		February	25	March	3
51	12	15	12	21	Abias		March	4	March	10
52	12	22	12	28	Jesua		March	11	March	17

Consuls, Olympics, Race Winners

In the preparation of a chronology grounded in facts, it is very useful to know who the Roman consuls were, as well as the year in relation to a given Olympiad and who the winners of the stadium race in that Olympiad were. Based on the sources referenced in the footnotes[67] [68] [69] [70], we have listed the following information for events around the Year Zero and the Year 33.

---

[67] https://en.wikipedia.org/wiki/List_of_Roman_consuls#1st_century_BC

[68] https://en.m.wikipedia.org/wiki/List_of_Olympic_winners_of_the_Stadion_race

[69] http://www.numachi.com/~ccount/hmepa/calendars/187.html

[70] https://en.m.wikipedia.org/wiki/32_BC

Events Around the Year Zero

AUC begins on April 21st	Julian Year begins on January 1st	Consul	Consul	Olympics.Year	Winners of the stadium race
750	-4	C. Calvisius Sabinus	L. Passienus Rufus	194.1	Demaratus of Ephesus
	replaced by	C. Caelius (Rufus?)	Galus Sulpicius		
751	-3	L. Cornelius Lentulus	M. Valerius Messalla Messallinus	194.2	
752	-2	Imp. Caesar Divi f. Augustu XIII (Jan–Aug)	M. Plautius Silvanus (Jan–Jun)	194.3	
	replaced by		L. Caninius Gallus (Jul–Dec)		
	replaced by	C. Fufius Geminus (Sept–Oct)			
	replaced by	Q. Fabricius (Nov–Dec)			
753	-1	Cossus Cornelius Lentulus	L. Calpurnius Piso	194.4	
	replaced by	A. Plautius	A. Caecina Severus		
	There is no year zero in the Julian calendar.	-	-		
754	1	Caius or Gaius Julius Caesar (Jan–Dec)	L. Aemilius Paullus (Jan–Jun)	195.1	Demaratus for the second time
	replaced by		M. Herennius Picens (Jul–Dec)		
755	2	P. Vinicius (Jan–Jun)	P. Alfenus Varus	195.2	
	replaced by	P. Cornelius Lentulus Scipio (Jul–Dec)	T. Quinctius Crispinus Valerianus		

Events Around the Year 33

The Date of the Resurrection

AUC begins on April 21st	Julian Year begins on January 1st	Consul	Consul	Olympics.Year	Winners of the stadium race
783	30	L. Cassius Longinus (Jan–Jun)	M. Vinicius	202.2	
	replaced by	L. Naevius Surdinus (Jul–Dec)	C. Cassius Longinus		
784	31	Ti. Caesar Augustus V (Jan–8 May)	L. Aelius Seianus	202.3	
	replaced by	Faustus Cornelius Sulla (9 May–Sept)	Sex. Tedius Valerius Catullus (9 May–Jun)		
	replaced by		L. Fulcinius Trio (Jul–Dec)		
	replaced by	P. Memmius Regulus (Oct–Dec)			
785	32	Cn. Domitius Ahenobarbus (Jan–Dec)	L. Arruntius Camillus Scribonianus (Jan–Jun)	202.4	
	replaced by		A. Vitellius (Jul–Dec)		
786	33	L. Livius Ocella Ser. Sulpicius Galba (Jan–Jun)	L. Cornelius Sulla Felix	203.1	Apollonius of Epidaurus
	replaced by	L. Salvius Otho (Jul–Dec)	C. Octavius Laenas		
787	34	Paullus Fabius Persicus (Jan–Jun)	L. Vitellius	203.2	
	replaced by	Q. Marcius Barea Soranus (Jul–Dec)	T. Rustius Nummius Gallus		

The Date of the Resurrection

Baptism of Jesus - painting by James Tissot

On November 6, 29, in the Gregorian calendar, equivalent to November 8, 29, in the Julian calendar and 13-Heshvan-3790 in the Hebrew calendar, Jesus Christ, at nearly 30 years of age, was baptized by

John the Baptist in the 15th year of Tiberius Caesar.[71] Jesus was about thirty years old when He began His ministry.[72]

On December 25, 29 of the Gregorian calendar, equivalent to December 27, 29 of the Julian calendar and 03-Tevet-3790 of the Hebrew calendar, Jesus Christ turned 30 years old, as he had turned 1 year old on December 25, year 0 of the Gregorian calendar.[73]

---

[71] http://www.dec25th.info
[72] Luke 3,23
[73] https://play.google.com/store/books/details?id=nSYEEAAAQBAJ

The Dates of the Jewish Passover

Pesach, the Jewish Passover, celebrates the end of Jewish slavery in Egypt. It begins on the 15th of the month of Nisan and lasts for 7 days. Since the days of the Hebrew calendar begin and end at sunset, Passover starts at sunset on the 14th of the month of Nisan.

According to the calculator on the website https://webspace.science.uu.nl/~gent0113/easter/eastercalculator.htm
The Jewish Passover in the year 33 occurred on Saturday, April 4th, in the Julian calendar, equivalent to April 2nd in the Gregorian calendar.

The Date of the Resurrection

Easter Sunday/Jewish Passover Calculator

Year (Anno Domini)	Show Gregorian dates before 1583	yes ▼
[−1] 0033 [+1]	Offset between Julian and Gregorian calendar	−2 days
Update calculator [C]	Julian Easter mode	Dionysian ▼

Dominical Letter	Julian reckoning	D	Gregorian reckoning	B
Lunar age parameters	Golden Number	15	Gregorian Epact	XII
Martyrology letters	Julian reckoning	q	Gregorian reckoning	m

Julian reckoning	Julian calendar date		Gregorian calendar date	
Easter Full Moon (*luna XIV*)	1	April	30	March
Easter Sunday	5	April	3	April

Gregorian reckoning	Gregorian calendar date	
Easter Full Moon (*luna XIV*)	1	April
Easter Sunday	3	April

Jewish Passover Feast	15 Nisan	3793	AM	Saturday	4	April

From Gregorian until Julian Easter Sunday	0 days
From Passover until Gregorian Easter Sunday	1 days
From Passover until Julian Easter Sunday	1 days

The Jewish Passovers During the Public Life

As we have seen earlier, the biblical records and chronology show that Jesus was nearly 30 years old when He began His public life.

In the Gospel of John, there are several mentions of the word "Passover" during the public life of Jesus.[74]

Let's check which these Passovers were:

AUC 783: from April 21, 29 AD to April 20, 30 AD

On 14 Nisan 3790, equivalent to April 3, 30 Gregorian and April 5, 30 Julian, the Jews observed the eve of the Feast of Passover, the Jewish Passover. It was the 16th year of Tiberius Caesar.

AUC 784: from April 21, 30 AD to April 20, 31 AD

On 14 Nisan 3791, equivalent to March 24, 31 Gregorian and March 26, 31 Julian, the Jews observed the eve of the Feast of Passover, the Jewish Passover. It was the 17th year of Tiberius Caesar.

AUC 785: from April 21, 31 AD to April 20, 32 AD

---

[74] John 2,13; 2,23 ; 6,4; 11,55; 12,1; 13,1; 18,28; 18,39 and 19,14.

The Date of the Resurrection

On 14 Nisan 3792, equivalent to April 12, 32 Gregorian and April 14, 32 Julian, the Jews observed the eve of the Feast of Passover, the Jewish Passover. It was the 18th year of Tiberius Caesar.

AUC 786: from April 21, 32 AD to April 20, 33 AD

On Thursday, March 31, 33, equivalent to April 2, 33 Julian and 13 Nisan 3793 Hebrew, after sunset on Thursday began the day of preparation for the Jewish Passover, which extends throughout Friday until sunset. Jesus and His disciples had the Last Supper before the crucifixion.

The Last Supper on Thursday

Last Supper – painting by James Tissot

G: March 31, 33, Thursday
J: April 2, 33
H: 13 Nisan, 3793

The Gospels of Matthew, Mark, and Luke record Jesus celebrating Passover before His death[75], but the Gospel of John records that the Jews were not celebrating Passover until the late afternoon of Friday.[76]

Did the term "Passover" apply only to the night when the Passover lamb was eaten, or was it also used for other occasions?

---

[75] Matthew 26,17; Mark 14,12; Luke 22,15
[76] John 18,28; 19,14

Raymond Brown and Jonathan Klawans[77] have suggested that the Last Supper was not a Passover meal. However, contrary to this hypothesis, the Gospel of Mark uses the term "Passover" four times in describing the preparations for the meal, and there is much agreement regarding the format and ritual of Passover.

Jesus Christ and His disciples held the Last Supper on Thursday, March 31, 33, after sunset, which means that the day of preparation for the Jewish Passover had already begun and would continue through Friday until sunset.

---

[77] Jonathan, Klawans, "Was Jesus' Last Supper a Seder?" Biblical Archaeology Society, 07 January 2014.

The Crucifixion on Friday

The Death of Jesus – Painting by James Tissot

G: April 1st, 33, Friday
J: April 3rd, 33
H: 14th of Nisan, 3793

In some translations of John 19:14, the trial of Jesus is described as taking place on the "day of preparation for the Passover." In Greek, the word used was "Paraskeve," which is the name for Friday.[78] For Jews, Friday is the day of preparation for the Sabbath.

Jesus Christ was crucified at the age of 33 years and 3 months on Friday, April 1st, 33, according to the Gregorian calendar, which corresponds to the 14th of Nisan, 3793, in the Hebrew calendar, the eve of the Jewish Passover.

Saturday, April 2nd, 33, according to the Gregorian calendar, which corresponds to the 15th of Nisan, 3793, in the Hebrew calendar, was the Feast of Pesach, the Jewish Passover.

On Sunday, April 3rd, 33, according to the Gregorian calendar, Jesus Christ was resurrected.

Since Jesus was crucified and died on Friday afternoon, that was the first day. At sunset on Friday, the second day began. Then, at sunset on Saturday, the third day began. Thus, Jesus truly rose "on the third day," on Sunday, the first day of the week.[79]

Christ had stated that He would spend three days and three nights in the heart of the earth, but

---

[78] Joy, John P. "Ratzinger and Aquinas on the Dating of the Last Supper: In Defense of the Synoptic Chronology," The New Blackfriars, Vol. 94.

[79] Matthew 20, 19 , Matthew 28,1-6.

according to most biblical scholars, this expression does not necessarily mean three full 24-hour periods. The expression "three days and three nights" refers to part of the period.

Jesus used the expression "on the third day" to refer to the time of His resurrection after the crucifixion.[80]

However, the expression "on the third day" does not mean "after three days."

Thus, Jesus died on the first day (Friday) and rose on the third day (Sunday).

The 24-hour period in Jewish time is counted from 6 PM to 6 AM. The 24-hour period in Roman time is counted from midnight to midnight.

The Jews divided the night into four parts called watches and the day into four parts called hours: The hour of prime lasted from sunrise until 9 AM. The hour of terce lasted until 12 PM. The hour of sext lasted until 3 PM. The hour of none lasted until sunset.

The evangelist John states that Jesus was on trial around the sixth hour of Roman time, which is 6 AM Roman time.[81]

The evangelist Mark states that Jesus was crucified at the third hour of Jewish time, which corresponds to 9 AM Roman time.[82]

The evangelist Mark states that Jesus died at the ninth hour of Jewish time, which is 3 PM Roman time.[83]

---

80 Matthew 16,21, Matthew 17,23, Matthew 20,19, Matthew 26,61
81 John 19,14
82 Mark 15,25
83 Mark 15,34-37

The Romans would leave the bodies of the crucified for the vultures, but the Jews insisted on burial. According to Jewish law, those crucified had to be taken down on the same day.[84]

Jesus was buried on Friday before 6 PM Roman time, which is when the Jewish Passover Sabbath began.[85]

---

[84] Deuteronomy 21,22-23
[85] Mark 15, 42-46

The Burial on Friday

On Friday, around three o'clock in the afternoon, Jesus died. There was an earthquake.

Among the women present were Mary Magdalene, Mary the mother of James the Lesser and Joseph, Salome, and the mother of the sons of Zebedee.

Although the soldiers confirmed that Jesus was already dead, one of them pierced His side with a spear.

As evening approached on that Friday, a wealthy man from Arimathea named Joseph, a disciple of Jesus, arrived. He went to Pilate and asked for the body of Jesus.

Pilate was surprised to hear that He had already died, so he summoned the officer and asked if Jesus had been dead for some time.

After receiving confirmation from his officer that Jesus was indeed dead, Pilate ordered that the body be handed over to Joseph of Arimathea.

Joseph took the body and carried it away. Nicodemus was also present, bringing spices.

They took Jesus' body and wrapped it in a clean linen cloth, along with the spices, according to burial customs. Then they placed Jesus' body in the new tomb that Joseph of Arimathea had had carved into the rock. After rolling a large stone over the entrance of the tomb, they left.

Mary Magdalene and the other Mary were sitting there, in front of the tomb, and saw where Jesus' body was placed. Then they went home.[86]

57

---

[86] Matthew 27,46-61; Mark 15,33-47; Luke 23,44-56; John 19,30-42

The Sabbath of the Jewish Passover

G: April 2, 33, Saturday
J: April 4, 33
H: 15/Nisan/3793

The Jewish Sabbath begins at sunset on Friday and ends at sunset on Saturday.
It is likely that Christ's disciples, on the day after His death, hid out of fear of the Jewish and Roman authorities.
The priests and Pharisees requested permission from Pilate to guard Jesus' tomb[87] to prevent His disciples from stealing the body.
The disciples spent the Sabbath in fear, still traumatized by the horrific events of Friday. Their hopes for the establishment of the messianic kingdom had been shattered. There was nothing to do on the Sabbath except rest.[88]
The Jewish leaders were also afraid due to the unusual circumstances surrounding Christ's death—the darkness at noon, the tearing of the Temple veil, the earthquake, and reports of the dead being raised (Jesus descended into the realm of the dead and freed them!). The Jewish authorities did not believe in Christ's resurrection but feared...

---

[87] Matthew 27,63-66
[88] Luke 23,56

The Sabbath, following the Friday of the crucifixion, was a day of exhaustion and fear, a day of waiting...

The Sunday of Christ's Resurrection

The Resurrection – Painting by James Tissot

G: April 3, 33, Sunday
J: April 5, 33
H: 16/Nisan/3793

According to Mark's account, which is the earliest account we have of the resurrection, when the Sabbath had passed, Mary Magdalene, Mary the mother of James, and Salome bought aromatic spices to go and anoint Him. Very early in the morning, on the first day of the week, they went to the tomb after the sun had risen. But they were asking among themselves: "Who will roll away the stone from the entrance of the tomb for us?" But when they looked, they saw that the stone, which was very large and heavy, had been rolled away. And when they entered the tomb, they saw a young man sitting on the right side, dressed in a long white robe, and they were afraid. But he said to them: "Do not be afraid; you are looking for Jesus of Nazareth, who was crucified. He has risen; He is not here. Look at the place where they laid Him. But go, tell His disciples and Peter that He is going ahead of you to Galilee; there you will see Him." And they fled from the tomb, and said nothing to anyone, because they were afraid...[89]

Jesus Christ rose from the dead, appeared to the disciples, spoke with them, ate with them, and allowed them to touch Him to see that He had risen in His entirety, body and soul, bearing the marks of the tortures He suffered and the nails in His hands.

---

[89] Mark 16,1-8

Many other people saw Him in the flesh after His death. It was not a mystical experience. Jesus Christ proved that His resurrection was physical.[90]

On this day, Jesus Christ, God incarnate, rose from the dead, thus conquering death and reopening the gates of eternity for the human race.

A wonderful event that deserves to be celebrated by Christians. It was the first Sunday after a full moon following the March equinox. And so, Christians decided to celebrate this special Sunday annually.

---

[90] Luke 24,39

The moon in April of 33

On the website
http://astropixels.com/ephemeris/phasescat/phases000
1.html

we see that the full moon occurred on Friday, April 3rd, 33, in the Julian calendar, equivalent to April 1st, 33, in the Gregorian calendar.

astropixels.com/ephemeris/phasescat/phases0001.html

Year	New Moon		First Quarter		Full Moon		Last Quarter	
0033					Jan 4	10:15	Jan 12	15:25
	Jan 19	16:10	Jan 26	07:52	Feb 3	04:22	Feb 11	07:43
	Feb 18	01:49	Feb 24	20:21	Mar 4	22:21	Mar 12	19:38
	Mar 19	10:39 T	Mar 26	10:34	Apr 3	14:52 p	Apr 11	03:46
	Apr 17	19:10	Apr 25	02:20	May 3	04:55	May 10	09:21
	May 17	04:00	May 24	19:16	Jun 1	16:20	Jun 8	13:51
	Jun 15	13:58	Jun 23	12:42	Jul 1	01:43	Jul 7	18:42
	Jul 15	01:57	Jul 23	05:39	Jul 30	10:07	Aug 6	01:15
	Aug 13	16:34	Aug 21	21:15	Aug 28	18:35	Sep 4	10:39
	Sep 12	09:43 A	Sep 20	10:58	Sep 27	03:51 p	Oct 3	23:52
	Oct 12	04:17	Oct 19	22:43	Oct 26	14:18	Nov 2	17:14
	Nov 10	22:35	Nov 18	08:45	Nov 25	02:04	Dec 2	14:02
	Dec 10	15:11	Dec 17	17:29	Dec 24	15:20		

On the website
http://www.paulcarlisle.net/mooncalendar/
we have the lunar phases for the month of April in the year 33 on the Julian calendar. Note that the full moon occurred on Friday, April 3rd, on the Julian calendar, which corresponds to April 1st on the Gregorian calendar.

www.paulcarlisle.net/mooncalendar/

April		0	0	3	3	AD
Sunday	Monday	Tuesday	Wednesday	Thursday	Friday	Saturday
29	30	31	1	2	3	4
5	6	7	8	9	10	11
12	13	14	15	16	17	18
19	20	21	22	23	24	25
26	27	28	29	30	1	2

New Moon
First Quarter
Full Moon
Last Quarter

Julian Calendar

Lunar Eclipse in April of 33

On the Friday of Christ's crucifixion, there was a darkness recorded in the Gospels.[91]

As we saw in the previous chapter, the moon was full that day.

The lunar eclipse catalog[92] points to this event[93] on Julian Day 1733204.116514, which corresponds to Friday, April 3, 33, in the Julian calendar, and April 1, 33, in the Gregorian calendar, according to the calendar converter.[94]

---

[91] Matthew 27,45; Mark 15,33; Luke 23,44-45

[92] http://www.eclipsewise.com/lunar/LEcatalog/LE0001-0100.html

[93] http://www.eclipsewise.com/lunar/LEprime/0001-0100/LE0033Apr03Pprime.html

[94] https://www.fourmilab.ch/documents/calendar/

The Earthquake in April of 33

The Earthquake – painting by James Tissot

There was an earthquake[95] when Jesus Christ died, around 3:00 p.m. on Friday, April 1, in the year 33 of the Gregorian calendar, equivalent to April 3, 33 in the Julian calendar, and to Nisan 14, 3793 in the Hebrew calendar, the eve of the Jewish Passover.

NOAA – National Oceanic and Atmospheric Administration, National Centers for Environmental Information, presents the following references to the earthquake of the year 33 in the Jerusalem region, latitude 31.800, longitude 35.200.[96]

---

[95] Matthew 27,45-51
[96] http://www.ngdc.noaa.gov/nndc/struts/form?t=101650&s=1&d=1

1853 - Mallet, Robert - Catalogue of Recorded Earthquakes from 1606 B.C. to A.D. 1850, Part I, 1606 B.C. to 1755 A.D. Report of the 22nd Meeting of the British Association for the Advancement of Science held at Hull, Sept., 1853, John Murray, London, p. 1-176.

1911 - Milne, John - Catalogue of Destructive Earthquakes [7 to 1899 A.D.], Report of the 81st Meeting of the British Association for the Advancement of Science, Portsmouth, London, United Kingdom, p. 649-740.

1985 - Alsinawi, S.A., S.G. Baban, and A.S. Issa - Historical seismicity of the Arab region. IASPEI/UNESCO Working Group on Historical Seismograms and Earthquakes, August 27-28, 1985, Tokyo; Preliminary Proceedings, p. 59-84.

1928 - Willis, Bailey - Earthquakes in the Holy Land, Bulletin of the Seismological Society of America, vol. 18, no. 2, p. 74-103.

1994 - Amiran, D.H.K., E. Arieh, T. Turcotte - Earthquakes in Israel and adjacent areas: macroseismic observations since 100 B.C.E. Isr. Explor. J., vol. 44, p. 260–305.

The Date of the Resurrection

The journal "International Geology Review"[97] published a study by geologists who concluded that Jesus Christ was crucified on Friday, April 3, 33 AD (Julian calendar). The geologists, led by researcher Jefferson Williams from Supersonic Geophysical, studied seismic activity in the Dead Sea region, 20 kilometers from Jerusalem. They analyzed soil samples from Ein Gedi Spa, geological records, and astronomical data.

---

[97] Jefferson B. Williams, Markus J. Schwab & A. Brauer (2012) An early first-century earthquake in the Dead Sea, International Geology Review, 54:10, 1219-1228, DOI: 10.1080/00206814.2011.639996

The Dates of Christian Easter

The feast of Easter, celebrating the resurrection of Christ, is observed on the Sunday following the first full moon after the March equinox, which occurs around March 20. If this full moon falls on a Sunday, then Easter is celebrated on the following Sunday.

Thus, Easter Sunday, depending on the year, can fall between March 22 and April 25.

On the website
http://www.truebiblecode.com/BLCTable.html
we see that in the year 33, the March equinox occurred on March 20 of the Gregorian calendar.

On the website
http://www.paulcarlisle.net/mooncalendar/
we have the Julian calendar for the year 33, where we can see that the first full moon after the March equinox occurred on Friday, April 3, which corresponds to April 1 in the Gregorian calendar. Therefore, the following Sunday was April 5 in the Julian calendar, which corresponds to Sunday, April 3, in the Gregorian calendar.

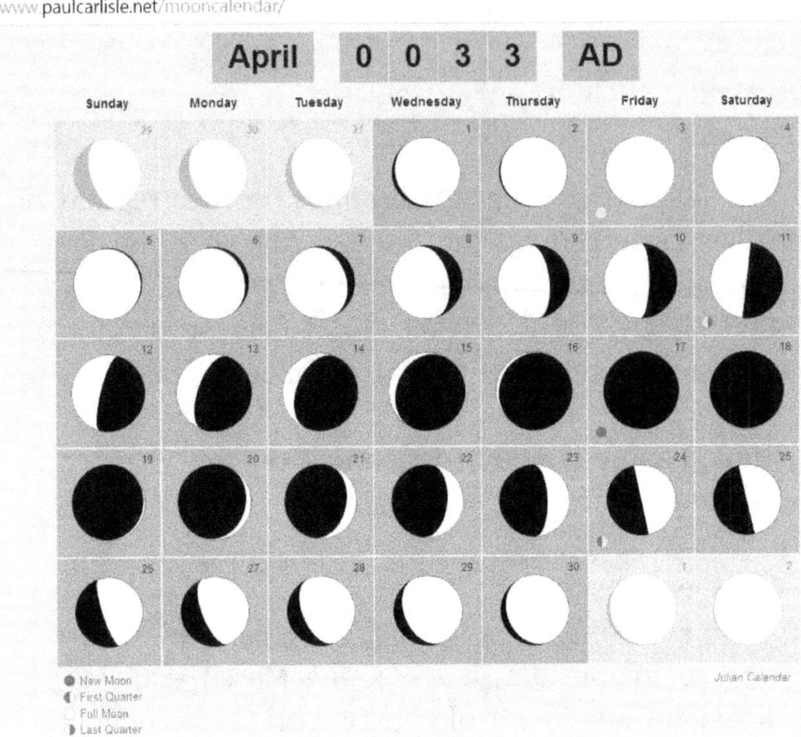

For the year 2020, when this book was first published, we see that the March equinox was on the 20th.
In 2020, the first full moon after the March equinox was on April 7, and the following Sunday, April 12, in the Gregorian calendar.

The Date of the Resurrection

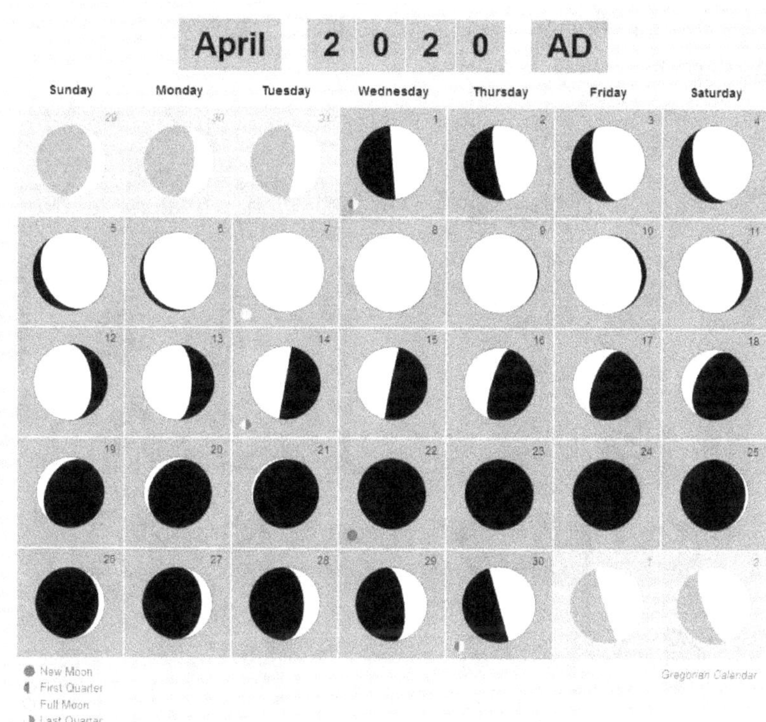

In the year 2021, the first full moon after the March equinox was on March 28, and the following Sunday was April 4.

www.paulcarlisle.net/mooncalendar/

March 2 0 2 1 AD

Sunday Monday Tuesday Wednesday Thursday Friday Saturday

New Moon
First Quarter
Full Moon
Last Quarter

Gregorian Calendar

The Ancient Traditions

Christians celebrate annually, on December 25th, the Nativity of Christ the Redeemer, and during Holy Week, the climax of the celebration is Easter Sunday of the Resurrection.

We see that the ancient tradition of celebrating Holy Week follows the Gospel records and remains faithful to the chronology. Christ died on the Friday before the Jewish Passover and rose on the third day, Sunday, the first day of the week.

Tradition holds that Christ was 33 years old when He died and rose from the dead.

Easter of the Resurrection is the greatest feast of Christendom. If Christmas is the feast of the Incarnation of the Divine Son, Easter of the Resurrection is the feast of the grace Christ won for all humanity, the passage from death to eternal life.

Faith in the Resurrection of the Whole Person

The Doubt of Thomas – Painting by James Tissot

The Apostle Thomas needed to touch the risen Christ in order to believe, and then he exclaimed, "My Lord and My God!"[98]

---

[98] John 20,27-28

The Date of the Resurrection

The people who lived during the time of Jesus Christ, who saw and witnessed His death and resurrection, spread the good news that Christ is alive and reigns. This message has been passed down from generation to generation, even to this day.

Jesus affirmed that, although people today have not seen Him as His contemporaries did, we believe in His death and resurrection, which makes us even more blessed.[99]

The Christian faith holds that, thanks to Christ's resurrection, humanity has been transformed, and from then on, after death, our bodies will be transformed into immortal ones. Every person will rise from death in an integral way, that is, with both an immortal body and an immortal soul.

---

[99] John 20,29

Justice, Altruism, Charity

Jesus Christ, the incarnate God, not only reopened the doors of eternity for humanity but also left us many teachings.

In the encyclical 'Caritas in veritate,' Pope Benedict XVI states:

'Charity surpasses justice because to love is to give, to offer to the other what is "mine"; but it never exists without justice, which compels us to give the other what is "theirs," what belongs to them by virtue of their being and actions. I cannot 'give' to the other what is mine without first giving them what is due to them by justice. Whoever loves others with charity is, above all, just towards them.'

In the encyclical *Fratelli tutti*, Pope Francis invites us all to be altruists of justice and charity in favor of both those close to us and those far away.

The dictionary teaches that the adjective "altruistic" is attributed to someone who is not selfish; who seeks to help others without putting their own interests first, to the detriment of others. It describes someone who contains or expresses altruism, selfless dedication, philanthropy. It refers to someone who dedicates themselves selflessly, expecting nothing in return. The noun "altruist" refers to someone who demonstrates altruism; someone who does not act out of self-interest; a philanthropist.

About the Author

 Décio Martins de Medeiros.
Electronics Engineer, graduated from ITA in 1975.
Engineer at NEC from 1976 to 1977.
Executive at HP/Agilent from 1977 to 2009.
Business management consultant from 2009 to 2020.
He participates in the blog 'Prazer Compartilhar' and the 'Clube de Autores'.
He has published several books:
https://sites.google.com/view/autordeciomartinsdemedeiros/books-in-english

The Date of the Resurrection